*Bernhard Johannes Schmidt*

AF205551

**PLAINTEXT compact**

# The ASPERGER Syndrome

# for Teachers

*Bernhard J. Schmidt*

PLAINTEXT compact
The ASPERGER Syndrome
for Teachers

ISBN: 978-3749469666

*translated from:*
*KLARTEXT kompakt*
*Das ASPERGER Syndrom für Lehrer*
*© 2015 Bernhard J. Schmidt,*
*ISBN: 9783739220086*

Production and Publishing:
BoD – Books on Demand, Norderstedt, Germany
Bibliographic information of the German National Library:
The German National Library lists this publication
in the German National Bibliography; detailed bibliographic
Data are available online at http://dnb.dnb.de.

# Table of content

# I. PREFACE

The number of diagnosed autists is growing very
strongly. And so it is no wonder that teachers are
increasingly confronted with Asperger autistics as
students (AS students). Although there are individual
references in various publications to difficulties of AS
students (e.g., sensory hypersensitivity) as well as
supportive options. But despite nearly 70 years of
research, there is a lack of a deeper understanding of
autism.

A "unified theory", an overall picture that explains
strengths as well as weaknesses of AS students and points
out auxiliary possibilities, was missing so far.

The aim of this volume is to present a new theory to
teachers in a compact form and to answer the following
questions:

- How can I distinguish autistic behavior from
  "simple closedness" or disinterest?

- Are there any behaviors that I as a teacher should
  definitely avoid?

- Where are the limits, when do I have to involve a specialist?

- Are there any tips and tricks that I can use to help autistics attend classes?

- Often I hear from colleagues, the student has no desire, is too lazy or similar. Could it be that at least every now and then autism hides behind such behavior?

The theory presented is based on results of both social psychology and brain research.

However, it should prove itself above all in the daily interaction in school.

And also this book is an expression of autistic communication, i. compact clear text. Further information as well as sources etc. can be found on my homepage

www.autismusberatung.info

and in the books listed in the Annex.

For reasons of comprehensibility, I present neurologically typical people / students (NT people, NT students) and autistic people / students (AS people, AS students) as a black and white image. In between, of course, are many shades of gray and many, if not all transitions are fluent. As unified as AS people are at a fundamental level of communication and interaction, they are so different in the expression of their personalities. So what are the problems and opportunities for promotion of an AS student, must be considered from case to case. However, a unified autism theory makes this view much easier.

The male name always includes the female as well. And even if among five AS-people is only one female, should not be forgotten despite a continuous male name that there are also female AS-people / students.

# II. INTRODUCTION

In school life, the rise of autism diagnoses raises questions like "is not it a fashion diagnosis?" And "is not that just an excuse?".
No question, both can of course apply.
But some of your students have always been autistic (in the sense set out here) - but so far without diagnosis. A fundamental problem also and especially for the school operation is to consider autism alone as a deficit. And although the diagnosis has gone from a division into Asperger and Kanner autism and "Autism Spectrum Disorder," autism has rarely been considered beyond a definition of "disorder." But autistic people also have a number of strengths that can be perceived and promoted.

## 1      Pervasive developmental disorder?

Is autism really a developmental disorder? Development is dynamic and takes place in a socio-cultural environment. The interaction and communication between the environment and AS students will therefore decide whether or not there will be a "disruption" of development.
AS students are different!

Not in the realm of intelligence, since they are at least in a normal range, so have no impairment of intelligence. But AS students communicate differently, perceive their environment differently, have a higher energy requirement ...

And AS students, like all other students, need a social environment for their development.

Over the years, the school will be an important social environment for AS students to learn and develop.

## 2    Impairment of social communication and interaction?

The key diagnostic criteria for autism are "Impaired social interaction and communication". However, although both interaction and communication always take place between at least two sides and the impairment is allegedly related to the "social" aspect, the results of social psychology have not been used to understand autism. This is probably because psychiatrists and researchers get to see autistics only as individuals, not - like you as a teacher - in a classroom.

However, social psychology has shown for decades that communication and interaction in people is not "social", but for the most part group communication (for example

Tajfel, Turner ...)!

This group communication is based on an in-group / outgroup differentiation.

And it is largely unconscious! (See, for example, John A. Bargh: "Social Psychology and the Unconscious: The Automaticity of Higher Mental Processes").

The unconscious group communication takes place via gossip as "grooming". About facial expressions, gestures, modulation of the vocal melody, imitation of and synchronization with the opposite ...

Through the unconscious communication and interaction group affiliation, sympathy and antipathy, hierarchy ... are communicated.

It serves the unconscious orientation on the group, as "autopilot".
AS people lack this unconscious group communication!

It is true that school and teaching serve to impart knowledge and (hopefully) the guide to critical thinking. But for the most part, school consists of a very intense form of (unconscious) group communication and interaction. Not only during the lessons, but also during the breaks.

**The problem of AS students is not intellectual, but consists largely in the absence of (unconscious) group communication and interaction!**

Why this is so, becomes clear when looking at "Default Mode" and "Task Mode".

# III. DEFAULT-MODE / TASK-MODE

In the brain, research using fMRI (Functional Magnetic Resonance Imaging) has identified two distinct networks, the "Task Positive Network" and the "Default Mode Network". These work like a changeover switch, which means that only one of them can be active.
The "Task Positive Network" serves to accomplish tasks and solve problems.
The "Default Mode Network", on the other hand, is active when there are no tasks or problems to manage.
Derived from this, I distinguish two behavioral states, the

- „Default-Mode" (DM) and the

- „Task-Mode" (TM).

Your NT students are mostly in the DM.
This is characterized by:

- unconscious group communication

- through gossip, imitation ...

- thereby unconscious orientation on the group

- resulting superficiality

- and conformity (e.g., in fashion)

Lesson is for NT students the unpleasant interruption (if it succeeds) of the default mode, which prevails in breaks, vacations and leisure.

But even in class, at least in part, the DM will occur. Yes, much of the instruction even builds (meaningfully) on imitation learning, ie part of the DM. The default mode is beside the unconscious communication and interaction above all also an energy saving mode. Imitation learning as well as the unconscious orientation on the group consume little energy. So only the many lessons are possible.

The DM is opposite the task mode (TM).
This is u.a. marked by:

- Interest instead of superficiality

- Emulation learning instead of imitation

- Solution orientation instead of group orientation

11

- high energy consumption (the active brain consumes about 25% of body energy and is as energy consuming as boxing)

- NT students are at least 70% in the DM and are difficult to pull in the task mode.

**By contrast, AS students are 100% in the TM!**

This has many consequences:

1.) AS students lack the "autopilot", that is the automatic orientation on the group.

2.) They lack the unconscious group communication and interaction as well as an in-group / outgroup distinction. That is why they are often marginalized or targeted for bullying.

3.) Due to the lack of the "autopilot" the energy requirement is very high.

4.) AS students do not learn about imitation, but about emulation, that means by (repeatedly) searching for their own solutions.

5.) AS students communicate only factual information and understand only such information.

A comparison of DM and TM as a table:

| Default-Mode DM | Task-Mode TM |
|---|---|
| „Autopilot" | - |
| Power Save Mode | Energy intensive |
| Imitation learning / over imitation | Emulation lerning |
| Group-orientied | Task- and solution-orientied |
| Superficiality | Interest |
| ▼ | ▼ |
| **NT-Students** >= 70% | **AS-Students** 100% |
| ▼ | ▼ |
| in-group / out-group | no-group |
| Prejudice | No prejudice |
| Conformity / Obedience | Heterogeneity |
| Unconscious Group-behavior | Freedom |
| „pretend play" | - |
| Synchronisation | No synchronisation |

# IV. HYPERSENSITIVITY

In addition to the lack of the default mode you can at AS humans additionally observe a "filter problem" with sensory perceptions. The absence of "filtering" means that sensory stimuli are perceived more strongly. AS students hear, see and smell better than NT students, but often without being aware of it.

On the other hand, an automatic suppression of disturbances such as the dripping of a tap, the ticking of a clock or the flickering of neon tubes ... is missing.

Thus alone the noise, smell and visual levels in the classroom can lead to a sensory overload of the AS student!

The filtering out e.g. the voice of the teacher against background noise, which is done automatically in NT children, consumes additional energy for AS students.

# V. CONSEQUENCES OF TASK-MODE AND HYPERSENSITIVITY

The absence of the default mode in combination with the hypersensitivity can have many problematic consequences :

## 1    Lack of energy

On the one hand AS students consume a lot of energy due to the lack of the "autopilot" and to filter the sensory environment. While the "battery" of NT students moves between light and dark green, in AS students the energy is more likely to diminish so much that it is in the red area.

## 2    Anxiety and stress

Secondly, the lack of unconscious group communication combined with sensory over-stimulation can cause anxiety and stress.
Yes, anxiety and stress are very often the main problems of AS students!
Due to the lack of unconscious orientation in the group, the behavior of the environment often appears irrational

and unpredictable.

An AS student must always consciously create an orientation himself.

In addition, AS students often experience exclusion and marginalization as well as bullying by their classmates. The DM, for example, during breaks and during the holidays, causes AS students stress unlike NT students. On the one hand, because the structures are lost and, on the other hand, because the rules and communication of the DM (gossip, imitation, for example, of fashion ...) are not mastered, group assignment is not understood.

## 3    Problematic behavior

First of all, AS students are, of course, children and adolescents with the same problems and conflicts as other children and adolescents as well. Not all problems of AS students are caused by autism.

But in addition, the following problems may arise:

### 3.1    Behavioral problems

Here are among others to call:

- Causing noises, stereotyped movements ...

- Encapsulation / retreat

- Aggressive behavior

Reasons can be:

- The battery is empty

- A sensory overload

- Anxiety and stress

or a combination of them. Sensory over-stimulation generates stress, stress in turn lowers the perception threshold, which leads to further over-stimulation and increased energy consumption.

Creating sounds or stereotyped movements and behaviors reduces stress. Creating (loud) sounds replaces the uncontrollable auditory environment with one controllable by the AS student.
A retraction or encapsulation is often caused by a (sensory) excessive demand (overload).
Aggressive behavior can be caused by both sensory overload and stress.

## 3.2    Learning Problems

As a matter of fact, AS students in TM, with interest and emulation learning, are almost ideal students - when it comes to learning critical thinking.

However, the lack of imitation learning can cause some problems in the classroom.

He is soaking up what interests an AS student. What does not arouse his interest, however, remains largely unnoticed.

The interest also leads to a very intense discussion of a topic, which may also stand in the way of progression in the class.

**AS students are but due to the task mode never "lazy"!**

Although AS students are always in the task mode, they are not always interested.

Possible causes of learning problems can be:

- The "battery" is empty, anxiety and stress, sensory over-stimulation ... fear and stress can lead to school refusal.

- Imitation learning is required - not emulation.

- Underload / overload.

- No interest in the topic.

- Look for other / own solutions - thus other time sequences. If the AS student has found the solution, it will no longer be recognized due to a new topic.

- Lack of understanding of tasks due to other communication.

- Missing feedback. Due to the lack of unconscious group communication, AS students need clear, factual feedback on their performance and behavior.

In summary, the social-psychological perspective as a graphic:

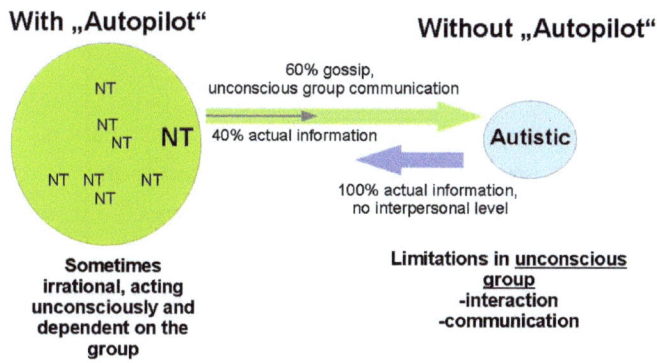

AS students therefore communicate very differently. They will express themselves (unless it concerns the specialty of the AS-pupil) much less. This can quickly be misinterpreted as disinterest.

Also, only things are reported that are perceived as not obvious and known. Behind it is the question "Why talk about things that are either known or anyone could easily derive?"

As a "problem solver" AS students lose interest as soon as the problem or task is solved.

# VI. TIPS AND TRICKS

Also you as a teacher are part of the class association, part of the group. And so you also take part in the unconscious group communication and expected it (until now unconsciously) from your students.

The absence of unconscious communication by the AS student does not mean a rejection or hostility. Even possible misconduct rarely has a really aggressive background, but rather is an expression of fatigue and / or despair.

Consider the AS student and his learning progress (also in social interaction) as an indicator of the learning environment.

## 1    In principle

Respect and acceptance of the AS pupil are indispensable prerequisites, strange and different as it may seem. Autism is another, not a worse way of being, communicating and interacting.

The school, the class association and the communication taking place there is a central and important place of

21

personal development for AS students.
Misunderstandings prevent the development and only lead to a developmental disorder.

Therefore, in consultation with the AS student and his parents, the education and training of teachers and also the classmates is important. This is the only way to avoid misunderstandings and to integrate the AS pupil. Understanding the nature and behavior of AS students reduces anxiety and stress.

Due to the lack of DM clear tasks are the royal route to participation in (social) events. For example, by selling drinks or cakes at the school festival, the AS student can participate in the event in familiar TM.

## 2     On autistic perception

Consider the perceptual peculiarities.
Pay attention to noise and disturbing background noise, light (too bright, flickering ...) and a "fuzzy" environment as well as smells. Reduce disturbing influences as far as possible.
Games on the perceptibility of the sensory organs with all pupils can sensitize them for the special perception of the AS-student.

Create a retreat where the AS student can recover and recharge their batteries.

Not being able to do is not synonymous with not wanting.

## 3    On autistic communication

Your communication usually corresponds more to a text task, the AS student of an equation. Communicate as clearly and concisely as possible. Avoid unnecessary and redundant information.

Talk to the AS student directly and give clear work assignments. Ask if the work order was understood correctly. The difference between DM and TM communication presents some hurdles and obstacles.

Provide a structure (such as temporal, spatial, etc.), at least until the AS student has learned to form his own structures.

Provide clear feedback on the results as well as the behavior of the AS student.

Avoid ironic or ambiguous remarks. For understanding, they need a "common ground", which is established by the AS student only through long-term participation in groups.

Give the AS student the opportunity to speak out when he does not understand something or feels mistreated.

If possible, adjust course contents and learning materials individually (emulation instead of imitation).

Teamwork can be difficult, but should always be practiced.

AS students often have self-esteem issues and are sometimes afraid of being judged by others. Do not force the AS student to lecture in front of the class, but encourage him.

# VII.     COMORBIDITIES

It should be clear that anxiety and stress are often the biggest problems for AS people. Due to the lack of unconscious group communication and interaction as well as the sensory hypersensitivity environmental stressors can cause some concomitant diseases. If such is present or suspected, the involvement of a suitable specialist is required.

Concomitant diseases can be or are common:

- social phobia

- anxiety disorders

- depressions

- health problems (stomach / intestines, skin, ...)

- selfharming behaviour

- ...

Also, be aware of exclusion and bullying of the AS student by classmates.

Not only the environment and fellow human beings cause anxiety and stress in AS students, but he causes these in case of doubt, even with his classmates.

The positive and negative development of AS people depends as much on the environment, society and groups as on NT people.

# VIII.    STRENGTHS

Already in 1999, Carol Gray and Tony Attwood published the "Criteria for the Discovery of Aspie" (the text is freely available on the internet in several places). The approach was to redefine Asperger syndrome not deficient but by defining positive traits.
Among the qualitative advantages Gray & Attwood named:

In the field of social interaction:

- Relationships with peers characterized by absolute loyalty and impeccable reliability.

- Free from prejudice based on sex, age or culture; Ability to accept others as they are.

- Expresses his own thoughts regardless of the social context or sticks to personal beliefs.

- ...

In the field of cognitive skills:

- Original, often unique way of problem solving.

- Extraordinary memory and / or memory of details often forgotten or ignored by others, such as Names, dates, schedules, routines.

- Enthusiastic perseverance in persevering in collecting and organizing information on a topic of interest.

- Persistence of thinking.

- ...

And additionally:

- Socially "unsung hero" with confident optimism: frequent victim of the social weaknesses of others and still clinging to the belief that real friendships are possible.

- A higher probability than in the average population to attend university after high school.

- Often caring to others outside the framework of typical development.

Unfortunately, however, this view was taken neither by the research nor by society.
Instead, one stayed with the deficit perspective.

For understanding and promoting AS students
In school, however, the perception and consideration of these positive aspects of Asperger syndrome is of central importance.

# IX. BIBLIOGRAPHY:

Schmidt, Bernhard J. (2015/1): Autistic and Society. An angry Change of Perspective. Vol. I: **Understanding Autism**. Norderstedt: Books on Demand.

Schmidt, Bernhard J. (2015/2): Autistic and Society. An angry Change of Perspective. Vol. II: **Support for Autistic**? Norderstedt: Books on Demand.

Schmidt, Bernhard J. (2016): Plaintext compact. **The Asperger Syndrome – Between Bullying and Inclusion**. Norderstedt: Books on Demand.

Schmidt, Bernhard J.; Ganz, Andreas (2016): Plaintext compact: **The Asperger Syndrome - not only for Psychotherapists.** Norderstedt: Books on Demand.

Schmidt, Bernhard J.; Döhler, Christiane and Deniz (2018): **Autism – Sexuality – Relationships.** Norderstedt: Books on Demand.

Schmidt, Bernhard J. (2019): **Autism and the Refrigerator Mother Myth. A Rehabilitation of Bruno Bettelheim.** Norderstedt: Books on Demand.

Schmidt, Bernhard J. (2019): Plaintext compact. **The Asperger Syndrome – for Parents.** Norderstedt: Books on Demand.

Schmidt, Bernhard J. (2019): Plaintext compact. **The Asperger Syndrome – for School Assistants.** Norderstedt: Books on Demand.

Schmidt, Bernhard J. (2019): Plaintext compact. **The Asperger Syndrome – for Physicians.** Norderstedt: Books on Demand.

Schmidt, Bernhard J. (2019): **Autism – Fight or Flight. New Perspectives on Challenging Behaviors.** Norderstedt: Books on Demand.